Drawn
to the Gospels
An Illustrated Lectionary

JAY SIDEBOTHAM

CHURCH
PUBLISHING
INCORPORATED

□ □ □

This book is dedicated to Frances,
who after many years of marriage remains kind enough
to chuckle at my cartoons.

□ □ □

Church Publishing
19 East 34th Street
New York, NY 10016
www.churchpublishing.org

Cover art by Jay Sidebotham
Cover design by Jennifer Kopec, 2Pug Design
Typeset by Denise Hoff

Library of Congress Cataloging-in-Publication Data

ISBN-13: 978-1-64065-080-0 (pbk.)
ISBN-13: 978-1-64065-081-7 (ebook)

CONTENTS

INTRODUCTION
How Would You
Tell the Story of Jesus?

What do you think is most important for people to know about Jesus? What part of the story would you emphasize? Evidently, telling the story of Jesus is something we're all supposed to do. In the service of Holy Baptism, the following question is asked of the whole congregation:

> Will you proclaim by word and example the Good News of God in Christ?

It is a promise that we will share the Good News of Jesus as we know it, a promise that we will tell the story. There are lots of ways to do that. This book is just one of them, as it moves us through the church year, beginning with the First Sunday in Advent. For each Sunday, we include the citation for the gospel to be read in church on the appointed Sunday, a few comments about the reading, some questions to think about, and a cartoon to illustrate something about the passage.

It's exciting that there's more than one way to tell Jesus's story. We give thanks in particular for the four gospels in the New Testament, and the varied ways that they share the story of Jesus.

What About the Cover of This Book?

For a long time, the church has recognized the distinctive voices of the gospels and represented them with ancient symbols: Matthew is represented as a human being, Mark as a lion, Luke as an ox, and John as an eagle. Each character is depicted with wings, indicating the presence and participation of God in the writing of the gospels. The symbols, depicted on the cover, have biblical roots. We read about four such figures in the Book of Ezekiel (chapter 1), and also in the Revelation to John (4:6–9ff).

As you might imagine, commentators over the centuries have offered various interpretations of these symbols, some more far-fetched than others. For example, the symbol of Matthew—a winged person, or perhaps an angel—represents the humanity of Jesus, noting the way the gospel begins with the genealogy of Jesus. The symbol of Mark—a lion—suggests a figure of courage and monarchy, as Jesus announces the nearness of the Realm of God. The symbol of Luke—an ox—reflects a figure of sacrifice, service, and strength. The symbol of John—an eagle—may represent the soaring, poetic language of the gospel, or the persistent and paradoxical theme in John's gospel that Jesus comes from above and returns to his heavenly realm when he is "lifted up"—lifted up on the cross, lifted up to heaven.

At various times in the history of the church, efforts have been made to harmonize, even homogenize, the gospels. The *Diatessaron*, a document created by an ascetic named Tatian in the second century, is one of the earliest examples of this kind of attempt. The church, over the centuries, decided to let four distinct voices stand, even if and when they disagree (and they sometimes do).

The church has also decided that it is important for us to hear each of these voices. So we worship on Sunday guided by a three-year cycle called the Revised Common Lectionary, which is a schedule of readings used by many denominations. On any given Sunday, you could drop in on a church down the street or on the other side of the globe and hear the same readings that are being read at your home church.

The lectionary is designed for a year-long focus on each of three gospels, Matthew, Mark, or Luke. They have been called the synoptic gospels, which literally means that they can be seen together, or alongside each other, in parallel tracks. (*Syn* is a prefix meaning with; *optic* has to do with being seen.) These three gospels follow a similar outline and share a great deal of material, though each one contains some unique material. In the course of the three lectionary years, we read a good chunk of the Gospel of John, which follows a different outline and represents both a different style of writing and a distinctive theological perspective on the story of Jesus.

Which Brings Us to the Gospel of Matthew . . .

This year in church, Year A, we will focus on the gospel attributed to Matthew. It's the first of four gospels, placed in order of priority at an early point in the history of the church. Scholars disagree about the reasons for that placement. Most agree that the second one, the Gospel of Mark, is the earliest of the gospels, and that the Gospel of Matthew and the Gospel of Luke used Mark as a basis for their writing, building on a basic outline and then adding other material.

What do we know about Matthew? Tradition holds that he was one of the twelve disciples, also known as Levi, a tax collector who was called by Jesus to discipleship. He's named in a number of places among the list of disciples and apostles. Whether the person described in Matthew 9:9 was the author of the book, or whether a person or persons assigned his name to this gospel, we may never know for sure. Since so much of Matthew reflects the timeline and language of the Gospel of Mark, it seems likely that Matthew is not simply writing a firsthand account.

Regardless of authorship (other books can argue about that), the message is distinctive. Our faith would be deeply diminished without this first gospel. We would, for instance, not know of the visit of the magi to worship the Christ child. We would not have the Sermon on the Mount all in one place. We would miss a number of important parables, perhaps most notably the story of the separation of sheep and goats in Matthew 25, a parable which has led the church to consider its call to serve those in greatest need, read on the last Sunday of the church year.

Whoever wrote this gospel, it presents a vision of Jesus in continuity with Moses. As there are five books attributed to Moses in the Torah (the first five books of the Hebrew Scriptures), so, in the Gospel of Matthew, there are five blocks of teaching by Jesus (also referred to as discourses), including the Sermon on the Mount, portions of which we'll read together in the coming year. This sermon, found in chapters 5–7, has had great influence throughout history, most notably in recent times in the loving, life-giving, liberating ministries of Mahatma Gandhi and Martin Luther King, Jr.

The gospel stresses the continuity between the Jewish tradition and the Jesus movement. Jesus does not come to abolish the law, but to fulfill it and, in some respects, to make it more rigorous. Of all the gospels, Matthew focuses most on the life of the church, which again, argues for a later date for the gospel. In a number of passages, the gospel describes ways for the church community to live together, and ways for church members to get along when disagreements arise. Apparently, church fights are nothing new.

As we move through the year, we'll highlight passages that are unique to Matthew, and note those which appear in other gospels.

Which Brings Us to This Book . . .

It is clear that, in the Christian tradition, spiritually vital congregations and spiritually vital individuals engage with the Bible on some level. The Prayer Book recommends that we read, hear, learn, mark, and inwardly digest scripture. You can find a prayer, a collect that instructs us to do that on page 236 of the Book of Common Prayer. We'll read that collect in November, on the second to the last Sunday of the church year. There are many ways to bring that prayer to life. This book and its companions for the other two years of the lectionary cycle offer just one way to go deeper with the gospel reading you hear on Sunday.

For each Sunday in the year, we include the citation for the gospel reading. You may want to have a copy of the Bible nearby. Episcopalians most often use the New Revised Standard Version in Sunday worship. We include a brief paragraph of commentary, followed by a few questions. On the left facing page, we add a cartoon drawing—one person's perspective on the story. Some of the cartoons are silly. Some are slightly irreverent. They are offered to bring the gospel passage to life, and they are offered with a light touch, in the spirit of G.K. Chesterton, who said that angels could fly because they take themselves lightly.

How to Use This Book

You might use this book for your own personal devotion, as a way to get ready for Sunday, or as a way to reflect on the gospel passage after you have been to church and heard a compelling, or maybe not so compelling, sermon. You might want to use the book in your home with those in your household. Perhaps after dinner, you might read the passage and answer a couple of the questions and then talk about the drawing, or even add to it.

You might want to copy the drawings and put them in the church bulletin, or have them on individual sheets or even posters, for children (of all ages) to color. You might use the book as a resource in Sunday School classes, Bible studies, or Confirmation classes. Some adults even seem to enjoy the drawings. Some may enjoy coloring them, since adult coloring books seem to be all the rage.

You may find the questions helpful, and you may need to translate them for use with different groups. If the questions provided are not working for you, here is another way to think about each gospel passage. Ask these two simple questions, which can be applied to almost any gospel passage:

1. Who is Jesus in this passage?

2. What does this passage tell us about what it means to be one of his followers?

You may want to simply read the gospel and ask about the so-what factor: What difference does this gospel passage make in my week?

Mother Teresa is revered and remembered for many reasons. Among her many vocations was a deep love of scripture. She taught that we are called to know the word, love the word, live the word, and give the word.

This book of often silly drawings is offered with the serious intent that the story of Jesus might become a part of who we are in a world that desperately needs to know more about God's grace and love. Our hope is that you will find this both enjoyable and edifying.

ADVENT

The First Sunday in Advent
Matthew 24:36-44

Notes on This Reading

Happy New Year! With this First Sunday in Advent, we start off the church calendar and dive into the Gospel of Matthew, which will provide most of the Sunday readings for the coming year. But we don't actually begin with the first chapter of Matthew. We start near the end, with a description of end times, or what we call apocalyptic writings. The word "apocalyptic" may convey doom and gloom, but it really suggests a revelation, as if a curtain is pulled back to reveal what's on the stage of a theater. With that in mind, consider what is being revealed in this passage. The word "look" is repeated throughout, and there's an element of surprise. Take this Advent season and the coming year to expect God to do something new, maybe even surprising, in your life.

Questions

1. What does the word "apocalyptic" suggest to you? Is it a good thing or not?

2. How is the coming of the Son of Man similar to events that surrounded the story of Noah?

3. How can you make yourself ready for what God wants to do in your life?

4. Have you ever been surprised by what God is doing in your life?

The Second Sunday in Advent
Matthew 3:1–12

Notes on This Reading

As we move further into the season of Advent, we meet John the Baptist. He gets a lot of airtime in the gospels and in the church calendar. That lets us know that he is important. We'll read about him this week and next. For this Sunday, we are introduced to his ministry in the wilderness, where he fulfills the promise of the prophet Isaiah as a voice crying in the wilderness, preparing the way of the Lord. Flannery O'Connor once said that the truth will set you free, but first it will make you odd. And John the Baptist was an odd one for sure. He wore strange clothes, followed a strange diet, and won a big following by calling his audience a brood of vipers. Mostly, he pointed beyond himself to the one who would baptize with the Holy Spirit and with fire, which may be part of the reason why he does indeed get so much attention.

Questions

1. Why do you think John the Baptist is so important in the gospels and in the church calendar?

2. What do you like about him? What do you find off-putting?

3. When he calls people to repent, what do you think he means? When have you had to repent? Does it help to know that the word really means to change direction?

The Third Sunday in Advent
Matthew 11:2-11

Notes on This Reading

Matthew is the only gospel writer that tells us of this poignant scene. John the Baptist has been tossed into prison. Early in his career, it seems that he bristled with confidence. Now in a prison cell, he sends word to Jesus asking deep questions. He asks whether Jesus is the one he should be following, or if they should look for another. It is as though he is asking if he had made a big error in following Jesus. Jesus affirms that John has not made a colossal mistake, noting the miracles of healing and liberation that are happening as a result of Jesus's ministry, signs that would accompany the arrival of the Messiah. After the messengers leave, Jesus speaks of John, claiming that there is no one greater born of a woman. Then, in a mysterious statement, he claims that such greatness is widely accessible, that everyone can be great.

Questions

1. How do you think John the Baptist felt in that first-century prison cell? What do you imagine the accommodations were like?

2. How was John to know that Jesus was the one to follow? What are reasons that you think Jesus is worth following?

3. Jesus speaks of John's greatness. What do you think are qualities that make someone great?

4. Reflect on this quote from Martin Luther King, Jr: "Everybody can be great . . . because anybody can serve. You don't have to have a college degree to serve. You don't have to make your subject and verb agree to serve. You only need a heart full of grace. A soul generated by love."

The Fourth Sunday in Advent
Matthew 1:18-25

Notes on This Reading

As we come to the end of the short season of Advent, we give thanks for the unique contributions of the Gospel of Matthew. Today's passage provides for us a portrait of Joseph. Take note of the ways Joseph is described in these verses. Consider the adjectives used to describe him. Focus on his actions and what they reveal about his character. Joseph gets limited attention in the other gospels, but Matthew tells the story of the dreams that guide him, and the angelic messengers that tell him to take Mary as his spouse. In the days to come, he will again be asked to follow the angel's advice and take his family to Egypt, fleeing the wrath of Herod. But more about that later. For now, give thanks for Joseph, a good man.

Questions

1. What are the ways that Joseph is described? What qualities does he exhibit? What does the author tell us about his character?

2. Reflect on the name prophetically assigned to this infant: Emmanuel. What is the significance of the phrase "God with us"? What did it mean for the first Christians? What does it mean for you?

3. Joseph has been described as someone who illustrates the adage: Life happens instead of what you plan. What does Joseph have to teach us about being ready to change plans? About going with the flow?

CHRISTMAS

Nativity of Our Lord Jesus Christ
Christmas Eve and Day
as well as Proper II
Luke 2:1-20

Notes on This Reading

We leave the Gospel of Matthew for this great celebration in the life of the church. We shift to Luke's gospel, which gives us the fullest account of the birth of Jesus. It's worth noting that two of the four gospels (Mark and John) don't tell us anything about Jesus's birth. But Luke shares the story of shepherds greeted by angels with hymns of praise and greeted by the innkeeper with a "No Vacancy" sign. Luke tells about the gathering for worship around the manger. It's a story of joy to the world.

Questions

1. This may well be the most familiar story in the New Testament. Try to read it as if you never heard it before. What strikes you? What puzzles you?

2. Why do you think the shepherds were the first to get the news of Jesus's arrival?

3. Since we've read about Joseph this year, what do you think he was thinking in all of this, as he gets the news that there is no room in the inn, as his wife gives birth in a stable, as shepherds show up? Did he get more than he bargained for? Does he provide any model for you in your journey of faith?

Nativity of
Our Lord Jesus Christ
Proper III and First Sunday after Christmas
John 1:1-14 (15-18)

Notes on This Reading

Christmas is more than a day. It's a season of twelve days, so we get another Sunday to celebrate the nativity of our Lord. The church gives us a totally different way to tell the story of Jesus's arrival, by directing our attention to the Gospel of John, which begins with a poetic prologue, much like an overture to a symphony. It will strike many of the themes of John's gospel and themes of the story of Jesus, describing the word made flesh dwelling among us, bringing light and life, grace and truth, facing rejection. Note how the prologue begins with the words, "In the beginning." Where else have you seen those words? It sounds like the author of this gospel wants to say that the story of Jesus is as significant as the story of Genesis. A new creation is happening.

Questions

1. What does it mean to you that Jesus is the word made flesh? In what sense is he the word?

2. How does he bring light? Have you ever experienced that enlightenment in your life?

3. What does it mean to be filled both with grace and truth? Do we need both those things?

4. Since we're reading the Gospel of Matthew a lot this year, with its emphasis on Jesus as the "new Moses," what does John's gospel have to say about Jesus compared to Moses?

Holy Name
Luke 2:15-21

Notes on This Reading

Our culture celebrates the New Year on January 1. On that same date, the church celebrates the Feast of the Holy Name, remembering the story in Luke's gospel of how Joseph and Mary brought the infant Jesus to the temple for presentation, in keeping with the Jewish tradition. That's a fitting feast to observe in this year when we read the Gospel of Matthew. One of the strong themes of that first gospel is the way in which Jesus comes to fulfill the tradition into which he was born and not to do away with it.

Questions

1. What is so important about a naming ceremony? How did you get your name?

2. What is important about the name Jesus? A variation on the name Joshua, it means "God saves." In what ways does the story of Jesus live into his name? Can you identify any way in which you have been saved? Any way in which you are being saved now?

3. Reflect on the traditions that were observed when you came into the world? What do you know about them? How have they affected the rest of your life?

Second Sunday after Christmas
Matthew 2:13-15

□ □ □

or Luke 2:41-52 *or* Matthew 2:1-12

Notes on This Reading

It's rare that there is a second Sunday in the season of Christmas, but thanks be to God, whenever that happens, the lectionary is prepared with a choice of three readings. There's the story of Joseph receiving another message from an angel (that's a little redundant since the word "angel" really means messenger). The angel tells Joseph to take his family to Egypt. There's the story from Luke about Jesus going to the temple with his parents as a twelve year old and lecturing the religious scholars of the day. And then there's the story of Epiphany and the magi coming from the east to worship the Christ child. These are various takes on Jesus's early years. We've provided a drawing for each of these stories. They set the stage for the beginning of his public ministry, described week after week in the upcoming season of Epiphany.

Questions

1. We read a lot about refugees in modern-day news. What does it mean to you that the holy family were also refugees escaping from a cruel and capricious tyrant?

2. What does it mean to you that Luke tells us Jesus grew in wisdom and stature? How could he be God among us and at the same time grow and change?

3. What insights do you get from the story in Luke about Jesus as a young teenager, teaching those much older than he is?

4. When we read the story of wise men coming from the east, do you wonder what they were looking for? What made them move?

EPIPHANY

The Epiphany
Matthew 2:1-12

Notes on This Reading

January 6 marks one of the great feast days of the church year, the Feast of the Epiphany. The feast launches a season that is really a series of stories that tell about the ways people come to see who Jesus is. We have Matthew to thank for the story that begins the season, the journey of magi from the east who follow a star to find the Christ child, and who bring gifts as an act of worship. One of the several messages of the season is that the Good News of Jesus is for all the world, knowing no geographical or national or racial boundaries. With the arrival of these wise ones, who were outsiders, we are assured that we are all welcomed to the community that follows and serves and worships Jesus, no matter who we are or where we come from or how far we have come.

Questions

1. The story is pretty familiar. Imagine that you have just heard it for the first time. What would strike you?

2. What do you make of Herod's role in the story?

3. Have you ever been on a spiritual quest, a journey like these wise men? What guided you in that journey? Was it a star? Was it your questions? Was it the need to stop and ask for directions? Was it another person who pointed the way? Take a look in your own spiritual rearview mirror and think about how you have been helped along the way.

The First Sunday
after the Epiphany
Matthew 3:13-17

Notes on This Reading

On the first Sunday after the Epiphany, no matter what year it is, we always read the same story: the story of Jesus being baptized by John the Baptist. It's easy to do since each of the gospels tells the story in its own way. We've already been introduced to John the Baptist during the season of Advent. Now he's back to baptize Jesus. Scholars and preachers have offered varied interpretations of why Jesus would or should be baptized by John, but one thing is clear: this important event not only serves as its own epiphany, a manifestation or a revelation of who Jesus is, but it also launches Jesus's public ministry through which he will bring his wisdom to the world. Heads up: in this year, and especially in this season of Epiphany, we will eavesdrop on Jesus's Sermon on the Mount, an important bit of teaching that reveals a lot about who Jesus is.

Questions

1. If you have been baptized, do you have any recollection of that event? If you were too young to remember, ask someone who was there to tell you about it.

2. What do you learn about the relationship between John the Baptist and Jesus in this story?

3. In your opinion, why was it important for Jesus to be baptized? Why was it important for each of the gospel writers to include the story?

4. Have you ever heard any voice telling you that you are beloved?

The Second Sunday after the Epiphany
John 1:29-42

Notes on This Reading

On this Sunday, we take a brief detour from the Gospel of Matthew to hear another version of Jesus's baptism from the Gospel of John, followed by the story of how Jesus called his first disciples. Note how John describes the baptism and what he saw. Note his own epiphany about who Jesus is. Then read on to hear Jesus as he asks prospective disciples, "What are you looking for?" Hear Jesus's invitation to them to "come and see." Think about what it means that Andrew claims from the brief encounter to have found the Messiah. What epiphany did he experience? There are all kinds of epiphanies going on in this reading!

Questions

1. What do you think it means that John describes Jesus as the Lamb of God?

2. What do you learn about John the Baptist's character in this passage?

3. Put yourself in the place of those first disciples. What do you think they saw in Jesus? What is it that you see in Jesus that makes you interested in following him?

The Third Sunday after the Epiphany
Matthew 4:12-23

Notes on This Reading

We return to the Gospel of Matthew, where we'll stay for a while, with stories describing epiphanies, the ways that people come to see who Jesus is. Right after Jesus's temptation in the wilderness (a story we'll read at the beginning of Lent), Jesus launches into his public ministry. The ministry is cast widely, crossing all kinds of boundaries, in keeping with the prophecy of Isaiah that speaks of a light dawning on those who have been in darkness. (If you want a cartoon image for the season of Epiphany, think of a light bulb going on over the character's head.) As Jesus begins preaching a message of repentance, which really means to change direction, he calls his first disciples, telling fishermen that they will now be fishing for people. It's remarkable how these disciples hear Jesus's call to follow him and immediately do so. It doesn't seem like they have to take a lot of time deliberating. Maybe that's something we could model.

Questions

1. Why does it matter that Jesus's ministry includes people who have previously been considered outsiders, people who were off limits?

2. How do you hear the word "repent"? Is it a positive or negative thing for you? Where do you need to change direction in your life?

3. What was it that made those first disciples drop what they were doing and follow Jesus?

4. What does it mean for us to be followers of Jesus today?

The Fourth Sunday after the Epiphany
Matthew 5:1-12

Notes on This Reading

For the remainder of Sundays in this particular season of Epiphany we will read excerpts from what may well be the most famous and influential sermon of all time. The Sermon on the Mount, as it has come to be known, is a collection of Jesus's teaching located in Matthew 5–7. The sermon begins with Jesus addressing a group of disciples on the mountaintop, offering teaching just as Moses delivered his teaching from Mount Sinai. By the time we get to the end of the sermon, multitudes are listening. It's always important for a sermon to have a good beginning. Jesus begins his sermon with the Beatitudes, an unusual and paradoxical list of blessings that come to people on the edges of life: those who are poor in spirit, meek, mourning, and persecuted. This is a great introduction to a sermon that offers surprising and often counter-cultural teaching.

Questions

1. As you read over the Beatitudes, pause and ask yourself: What is blessed about each of these situations?

2. What does it mean to be blessed anyway? What synonyms can you think of?

3. What do you think it means to be poor in spirit? Look up other translations to get some clues.

4. What do you imagine listeners thought when they heard this list of blessings?

The Fifth Sunday
after the Epiphany
Matthew 5:13-20

Notes on This Reading

We continue to make our way through the Sermon on the Mount. On the heels of the Beatitudes, Jesus speaks to his disciples about what it means to put faith to work in the world, what their calling will look like. He says that they are to be salt and light. He gives some clues about what those metaphors mean, but doesn't describe them fully, leaving ample space for the imagination of the reader. Whatever was intended with these images, it is clear that the disciples are intended to be distinctive and to make a difference in the world. How are you doing that?

Questions

1. Talk about the image of salt. What does salt do? (Note: There's not just one answer.) How are disciples to be salt, given what you've discussed?

2. Talk about the image of light. What does light do? How are disciples to be light, and what does the reading say about the intention of their shining forth?

3. What does it mean that disciples will be a city on a hill?

4. Have you ever hidden your light under a bushel?

5. How can you be salt and light this week?

The Sixth Sunday
after the Epiphany
Matthew 5:21-37

Notes on This Reading

Our journey through the Sermon on the Mount continues with interesting examples of how Jesus interpreted the scriptures of his tradition. Hardly a biblical literalist or rigid interpreter, he begins by noting what the tradition says about issues like murder, adultery, and divorce. Then with striking authority, he gives his own spin on these ancient teachings. He provides a much more rigorous teaching that seems to indicate that what really matters is what's in the heart. It's not just evil action that needs to be condemned, but evil intention. He sets a high bar indeed.

Questions

1. What would you say about the way Jesus reads his scriptures? What lessons are there for us in the way we read scripture?

2. What do you think about the way Jesus interprets laws of murder? Is anger in the heart as bad as murder? Does he really mean that?

3. Similarly, what do you think about the way Jesus interprets laws against adultery? He seems to take a strict approach. What do you make of it?

4. Finally, as he weighs in on divorce, and as we live in a culture where divorce is common, how do we apply Jesus's teaching here?

The Seventh Sunday
after the Epiphany
Matthew 5:38-48

Notes on This Reading

Jesus continues with more interpretation of the scriptures of his tradition. Again, he expresses an expansive view, looking at the intention of the law. We may have heard the phrase "eye for an eye" and interpreted it as permission to seek revenge. Jesus seems to be describing something else, a path not marked by retribution but by limits. If you are planning retribution, go no further than the wrong that has been done to you. And in fact, take the opportunity to do something totally counter-intuitive. Citing texts that speak of loving neighbor and hating enemy, Jesus issues the challenging call to love enemies. Finally, he talks about a call to be perfect, to be whole, as our Father in heaven is whole. This is no cheap grace here. The call to discipleship is rigorous. It is costly grace.

Questions

1. How would you describe the meaning of the phrase "eye for an eye"? What do you think Jesus meant by citing it?

2. Have you ever been tempted to go for revenge? What do you think the Sermon on the Mount would say about that?

3. How hard is it to love your enemies and pray for them? Have you ever had to do that? Give it a try today.

4. How do you interpret Jesus's call to be perfect as our Father in heaven is perfect? Aren't we all sinners? What kind of perfection do you think Jesus has in mind?

The Eighth Sunday
after the Epiphany
Matthew 6:24-34

Notes on This Reading

As we continue through the Sermon on the Mount, we skip over a few verses that we will read on Ash Wednesday. In the beautiful passage before us today, Jesus invites us to think about who it is we serve. As Bob Dylan sang a number of years ago, "You gotta serve somebody." Jesus then calls his disciples to a way of life free of anxiety, taking cues from the birds of the air and from the lilies of the field, all part of God's creation. They are all apparently able to trust in God's provision and to live their lives in full expression of God's creative intention, free of anxiety. That sounds pretty good. It's not a bad way to live.

Questions

1. Which masters do you serve in your life? Wealth? Status? Education? Parental approval? The approval of children?

2. What are ways that you cope with worry and with anxiety?

3. What lessons can be learned from the birds of the air?

4. What lessons can be learned from the lilies of the field?

The Last Sunday
after the Epiphany
Matthew 17:1-9

Notes on This Reading

We turn on this last day of the season to a story told in the first three gospels and always read on this Sunday. It's the story of the Transfiguration, a mysterious trip to the mountaintop. It is celebrated with its own feast day in the church calendar, August 6. Jesus once again ends up on a mountaintop, accompanied by a few close disciples, where a grand mystical experience unfolds. Think special effects like Steven Spielberg. Moses and Elijah appear with Jesus, and, in a way that is reminiscent of his baptism, a voice speaks from heaven. Jesus is called beloved by God. While Peter wants to capture the moment, Jesus insists that they cannot stay on the mountaintop. They must keep moving, in this case, making their way to Jerusalem for Holy Week. The church lives out that movement in its observance of the season of Lent, which will begin in just a few days.

Questions

1. What is so important about mountaintops? When have you had a mountaintop experience? Did you want to stay there or were you ready for it to be over?

2. Think about the disciples' various reactions to this incident. How would you have reacted?

3. Why did Moses and Elijah show up?

4. What is so important about a voice saying Jesus is beloved? How does that compare to the voice heard at Jesus's baptism, on the First Sunday of the season of Epiphany?

5. Do you have any idea why Jesus told the disciples not to tell anyone about this amazing event?

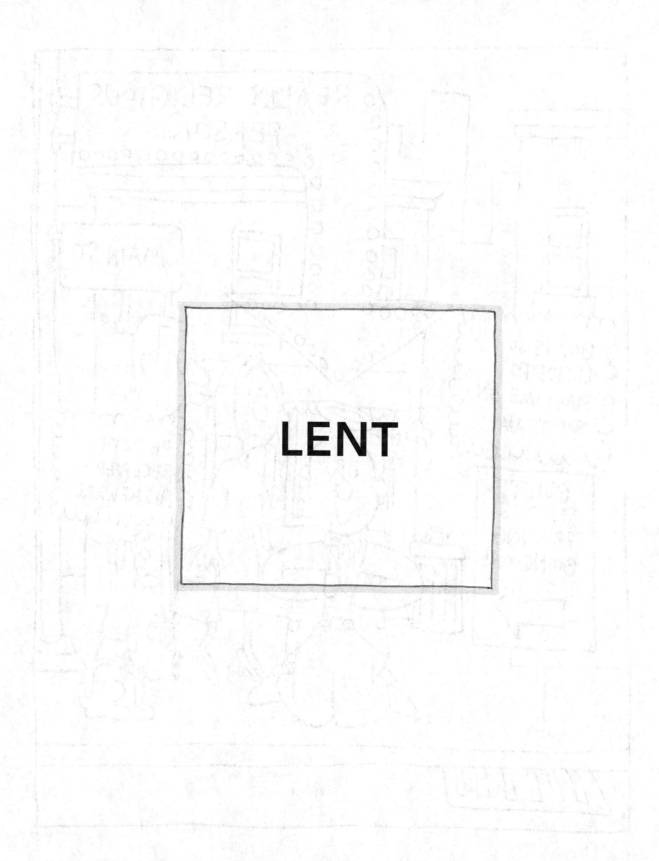

LENT

Ash Wednesday
Matthew 6:1-6, 16-21

Notes on This Reading

As we move from the season of Epiphany into the season of Lent, we return to the Sermon on the Mount, portions of which we read earlier this year. In that sermon, Jesus teaches his disciples about ways to observe religion. That's especially appropriate material to consider as we begin a season marked by repentance, self-examination, and spiritual growth. Jesus counsels his disciples to be on guard against hypocrisy. He warns against worrying too much about what people think of them. Jesus challenges listeners to think of motive, about where they are giving their hearts. In a challenge to his audience, then and now, he says where your treasure is, there will your heart be also. Sit with that thought this week.

Questions

1. What does this passage say to you about observance of religion? How does it help you as you begin the season of Lent?

2. What are ways that you can pray with greater authenticity?

3. Take some time this week to think about where you find your treasure. How does that correspond to where you are giving your heart?

First Sunday in Lent
Matthew 4:1-11

Notes on This Reading

Every year, on this first Sunday in Lent, we read a story told in each of the first three gospels. Right after his baptism, Jesus goes into the wilderness where he encounters the devil. After Jesus fasts for forty days, the tempter puts him to the test. The proposals? Turn stones to bread so you are not hungry. Throw yourself off the top of the temple and see if God actually comes through and saves you. Worship me and you'll have everything you need. The tempter likes to use scripture, which is what caused Shakespeare to write, "Even the devil can quote scripture." Jesus responds with his own citation of scripture, causing the devil to leave him, at which point angels come to wait on him. It is clear that the desert is not only a place of challenge and isolation but also a place of formation. Jesus is now ready to begin his public ministry.

Questions

1. When have you been in the wilderness? What did it feel like? What tests did you encounter there?

2. What does this story teach us about how we use scripture?

3. When you were in the wilderness, when you were being tested, did you ever find that it was also a place of formation, that you came out a different and maybe better person than when you first went into the wilderness? Share that story with someone this week.

Second Sunday in Lent
John 3:1-17

Notes on This Reading

From the earliest days of the church, a series of stories from the Gospel of John were read during Lent, which has always been a season that was partly about preparing for baptism on Easter. These stories were especially appropriate for that process of preparation—in churchy terms, a catechetical process. On this Sunday, we read about Jesus's night-time meeting with Nicodemus, a religious leader. Scholars have wondered why Nicodemus came to see Jesus at night. Was he really busy? Was he scared to be seen with Jesus in public? We don't know for sure. As in the other conversations that will follow in the rest of Lent, Nicodemus doesn't always seem to know what Jesus is talking about. When Nicodemus asks how an old man can be born again, the reader knows Jesus is talking about another kind of birth. Nicodemus will show up a couple more times in the gospel, including when Jesus's body is taken off the cross and laid in a tomb. For all his questions, he ends up a devoted follower.

Questions

1. Based on the questions he asks Jesus, what impressions do you have of Nicodemus? Why do you think he sought out Jesus at night?

2. What does it mean to be born from above or born anew or born again? Have you ever had an experience like that? Does it just happen once?

3. John 3:16 is one of the most famous verses in the Bible. You can find it in football stadiums, on billboards, on tattoos. Why do you think it's so important? Read it along with John 3:17 and see if that shifts its meaning for you?

Third Sunday in Lent
John 4:5-42

Notes on This Reading

Jesus met the woman at the well, and as the song says, "he told her everything she'd ever done." It's an amazing exchange, found only in the Gospel of John. It's a meeting that shouldn't have happened for many reasons. In that culture, a man was not to talk to a woman alone. A Jew was never to talk with a Samaritan. A holy teacher should avoid a woman with questionable ethics, and this woman had been married five times and was now living with someone who wasn't her husband. But that doesn't seem to stop Jesus. The conversation at the well goes deep, as Jesus speaks of himself as the living water. The woman represents all of us, bringing not only her initial cluelessness about what Jesus means, but also bringing her deep thirst of the soul. This passage includes wonderful and mysterious comments about the ways we worship. It's one in a series of rich, transformative encounters that guides us through Lent.

Questions

1. What strikes you about this meeting, Jesus alone at the well with this woman?

2. How is Jesus like living water?

3. What do you take away from the discussion of worship in this conversation?

4. How is this woman changed by her encounter with Jesus? How do you think her community reacted to the change?

Fourth Sunday in Lent
John 9:1–41

Notes on This Reading

We continue our way through the season of Lent with more stories of Jesus's one-on-one encounters with people. In this passage, Jesus meets a man who was born blind. The disciples want to turn him into a case study, an object lesson, a theological discussion point, asking whether he had sinned or his parents had. Jesus refuses to get sucked into that game. Instead, he heals the man, starting a conversation about what it really means to see. This miracle is one of the signs that marks Jesus's ministry in the Gospel of John, in this case signifying that Jesus himself is the light of the world. The story raises the question of who really has sight and who really is blind. It turns out the blind man comes to see, while religious leaders of the day reveal their own spiritual blindness.

Questions

1. What does it mean that Jesus is the light of the world, a theme we heard at the beginning of the gospel?

2. What does it mean to be spiritually blind? How do we come to spiritual vision? When have you gained insight?

3. How is it that people who claim to see may actually be those who are blind? How do we come to recognize our own spiritual blind spots?

Fifth Sunday in Lent
John 11:1-45

Notes on This Reading

This Sunday, we read one more rather lengthy gospel passage, the last of the signs described in the first half of the Gospel of John. The first sign was the miracle at a wedding in Cana, as Jesus turned water into wine. This last sign, the most dramatic, involving resurrection, is the raising of Lazarus from the dead. Once again, Jesus describes himself using that powerful phrase, "I am," an echo of the name for God in the Hebrew Scripture. (The name YHWH can be translated "I am who I am.") Jesus enters into the suffering of his good friends, Mary and Martha, who have just lost their brother. We note Jesus's tenderness of heart. Scripture tells us that Jesus wept at the death of his friend, and perhaps at the grief that his friends were experiencing, and maybe at the devastating power of death in human lives. He then declares his power as the resurrection and the life. He calls for Lazarus to be released from the bonds of death. As we come to the end of this season of Lent, it is a powerful preview (maybe something like coming attractions at the cinema) for the culmination of Holy Week, which is Easter morning.

Questions

1. Lazarus's sisters tell Jesus: "If you had been here, my brother would not have died." Have you ever wondered where God's power has been when you needed it?

2. What do you make of Jesus's emotional connection in this moment, with the poignant verse: Jesus wept?

3. What does Jesus mean when he says: "I am resurrection and I am life"? In what ways have you experienced that resurrecting power?

4. The word "resurrection" literally means "to stand again." Have you ever had that experience in your life?

Palm Sunday
Liturgy of the Palms
Matthew 21:1-11

Notes on This Reading

We begin Holy Week each year with a great parade, a procession of palms that recalls Jesus's triumphal entry into Jerusalem. The story is told in each of the gospels, which is one way we know of its importance. The story told in Matthew is filled with the fulfillment of scripture from the Old Testament. It's a great celebration, a declaration that Jesus is a king. We'll find out in short order that he may not have been quite the kind of ruler people expected. We'll learn (as if we needed to be taught) that human affections and allegiance are fleeting. In just a few days, Jesus's popularity, signaled in shouts of "hosanna," gives way to cries for his crucifixion, yet another indication of fickle human nature.

Questions

1. What does it mean to you that Jesus is king?

2. If you were in that crowd, do you think you'd be shouting "Hosanna"?

3. What kind of king do you think Jesus represented for the people of Jerusalem? Do you think of him as a king now? Is kingdom language meaningful in our day? Is there other language that might be more helpful?

4. Why do you think the mood of the crowd shifted so quickly?

Palm Sunday
Passion Narrative
Matthew 26:14-27:66

□ □ □

or Matthew 27:11-54

Notes on These Readings

It's been said that the gospels are really passion narratives with long introductions, which is to say that the gospels are not biographies. They do not cover every detail of Jesus's life. Rather they focus on the last week of Jesus's life. All that has come before (the stories of his birth, the miracles, his teaching) simply sets the stage for an exploration of the meaning of Jesus's death and resurrection. With that in mind, on Palm Sunday we read long passages of the gospel, telling the story of Jesus's last hours. In many churches, in keeping with ancient tradition, the reading is read in parts, as a drama. That is not only to keep the interest of the congregation. It is to say that this drama is actually something in which we all participate. Take this Sunday as an opportunity to enter into the story, and to think about where you fit into that story.

Questions

1. What do you think of the idea that the gospels are really focused on the last week of Jesus's life, that the story of his birth and the teaching and the miracles are all prologue?

2. Where do you see yourself in the passion narrative? Which character do you identify with? Which characters seem to engage in inexplicable behavior?

3. How does the reading of this long passage help to prepare you for a journey through Holy Week? What are your hopes for this distinctive week?

Maundy Thursday
John 13:1-17, 31b-35

Notes on This Reading

The word "maundy" doesn't get a lot of use in our culture apart from Holy Week. It is derived from the Latin word for command (mandatum) and points us to the new commandment that Jesus gave to his disciples at the Last Supper on the last night he was with them before he went to his arrest and trial and crucifixion. That commandment was summed up in a call to love others as God has loved us. It came not only in verbal instruction, but also in a compelling demonstration—the washing of the disciples' feet. And then Jesus instituted the meal by which we still remember his death and resurrection, the eucharist, with bread blessed and broken for us.

Questions

1. What does it mean to you that on the night before he died, Jesus offered thanks to God by instituting the eucharist, which is a word that really means thanksgiving?

2. In this Holy Week, how might you live into the new commandment that Jesus offered? What will that look like for you?

3. Is it possible to command love?

Good Friday
John 18:1-19:42

Notes on This Reading

What's so good about it? Some have said it was originally called "God's Friday." Others point to the goodness that shines through as Jesus stretches arms of love on the hard wood of the cross to draw us into his saving embrace. For this day, we again read the Passion Narrative, the story of Jesus's last hours, as recorded in the Gospel of John. It includes a number of distinctive features, as Jesus comes to the hour of glory he has predicted. It is the glory of the offering of self that is in the character of God. Jesus comes to that moment he has predicted, when he is lifted up. We'll find in short order that Jesus was probably referring not only to the moments lifted on the cross, but also to his exaltation to be with God. Often this long passage is read in parts, a repeat of what we did on Palm Sunday, not only to make a long passage more engaging, but also to cause us to consider who we are in the story. Were you there when they crucified our Lord?

Questions

1. What is distinctive for you in John's telling of this story? Do you notice anything different from what we read on Palm Sunday?

2. What do you make of the exchange between Jesus and Pilate? What picture of Pilate do you get? Why did he ask: "What is truth?"

3. Describe Jesus's demeanor as he suffers on the cross. What are his concerns?

4. Commentators have suggested that this version of the Passion Narrative bears responsibility for anti-Semitic attitudes and behavior in the church. Can you see how that might be true? What might we do to combat or correct that?

5. Having read this long passage, why do you think we call this Friday good?

Holy Saturday
Matthew 27:57-66

□ □ □

or John 19:38-42

Notes on These Readings

For this holy day—a day of rest and a day of quiet—we are offered two different passages from the gospels, one from Matthew and one from John. Both describe the hours after Jesus's death, as he is taken down from the cross. Both describe the loving and attentive ministry of Joseph of Arimathea. In the case of John's gospel, Nicodemus also appears. Remember, we met him earlier this year, in Lent, when he came to meet Jesus at night. Take this day as a day of quiet remembrance. Let words be few.

Questions

1. What do you think motivated Joseph of Arimathea to go public in his attentiveness to Jesus? Do you think that took courage? What was he risking?

2. How will you observe this particular feast day in the church? What will you do to carve out some silence?

3. Only Matthew includes details of a rumor that Jesus's disciples would steal his body. Why do you think that's included in this reading?

EASTER

Easter Vigil
Matthew 28:1-10

Notes on This Reading

The Easter Vigil offers one of the greatest liturgies of the church year. It has a bit of everything. It begins in darkness, with readings that recall God's saving history, with special focus on the story of the Exodus and the affirmation that Easter is indeed a new kind of Passover. In many ways, the Vigil reverses the path of the Palm Sunday narrative, which moves from the great celebration of Jesus's entry to Jerusalem to the tragedy of the cross. In contrast, the Easter Vigil moves from darkness to light, with the first declaration of alleluias and the first Eucharist of the Easter season.

Questions

1. How is Easter a movement from darkness to light?

2. How does the story of Jesus's resurrection seem similar to the story of the Passover and the Exodus?

3. As you read the passage from Matthew, how do you imagine the women who first saw Jesus felt?

Easter Day

John 20:1-18

□ □ □

or Matthew 28:1-10

Notes on These Readings

On this important day, we have a choice of readings. For those who wish to continue to learn from Matthew, the passage read at the Easter Vigil is offered. (See the previous entry on page 69.) Others may wish to hear the story as told in John, which includes the story of Peter and John racing to the tomb after hearing the news from Mary that the stone in front of the tomb had been rolled away. John gets there first, but Peter runs right in. Matthew makes a big deal about the linen cloths lying there. Consider why these particular and divergent details are mentioned in the gospels.

Questions

1. How important is it that the first witness in the resurrection stories is Mary Magdalene?

2. Peter and John run to the tomb. What does the narrative say about each one of them?

3. What do you think is the significance of the linens lying there?

4. Apparently, the disciples don't quite understand what has happened. Why do you think the gospels describe this gradual process of coming to understand the truth of the resurrection?

Easter Evening
Luke 24:13-49

Notes on This Reading

Because Easter is one of the days in the year when our churches are most full, one of the days when there are multiple services, the lectionary provides various versions of the resurrection story. On Easter evening, we have opportunity to read a passage that will come up again in a few weeks. It's the story of the disciples on the road to Emmaus. It is a story about how they gradually come to see who Jesus is. As in many other Easter accounts, it takes a little bit of time for the disciples to realize that Jesus is alive. That can be true for disciples these days as well.

Questions

1. What does it mean that the disciples are accompanied by Jesus on the road and they don't recognize him?

2. Is there any significance for you in the fact that the disciples walk with Jesus for a while before they actually figure out who he is?

3. What is the moment of recognition in the story? What has caused you to recognize who Jesus is?

Second Sunday of Easter
John 20:19-31

Notes on This Reading

Every year on this Second Sunday after Easter, we read about Thomas of doubting fame. It is a recognition that while there was wonder and amazement among those who first saw Jesus after the Resurrection, there was also a good deal of doubt, skepticism, and confusion. For some people, there was gradual realization that the Good News of Resurrection was true. It didn't happen instantly for everyone. While it might seem like a bit of a downer to speak of doubt on the heels of last week's great celebration, the Good News in the message is that doubt is okay. Frederick Buechner said that doubt is the ants in the pants of faith. It can lead to the kind of deeper faith that Thomas discovered when he finally saw the risen Jesus and said, "My Lord and my God."

Questions

1. What's your impression of doubting Thomas?

2. Why do you think that the stories of resurrection include so many occasions when people doubted? Wouldn't it have been better to edit out those stories?

3. What has caused you to believe? What has been convincing? What has triggered your doubts? Have those doubts been resolved?

4. Do you believe because of what someone has told you, or do you have to see for yourself?

Third Sunday of Easter
Luke 24:13-35

Notes on This Reading

The story of the road to Emmaus is told only in the Gospel of Luke. We owe a great debt to Luke because it's one of the most beautiful, poignant stories in the gospels. Two disciples leave Jerusalem after Jesus has died. They are dispirited and disappointed. They speak of how they had hoped that Jesus was the one they had waited for. Their grief blinds them to Jesus's presence with them on the road. As they travel toward Emmaus, Jesus teaches them about what his life and death meant. They invite him to join them for dinner when they arrive at their destination. Mysteriously, as the invited guest, he becomes the host, breaking and blessing the bread. At that point, the disciples realize that Jesus had been with them. They run back to Jerusalem to share this amazing news.

Questions

1. What are the range of emotions that these disciples might have been feeling as they left Jerusalem? What might they have thought about their time with Jesus?

2. Why do you think they didn't recognize Jesus?

3. The meal that they all share that evening sounds in many ways like the eucharist. Do you think that is coincidence or is it intentional?

4. Has the eucharist ever made it possible for you to see Jesus more clearly?

Fourth Sunday of Easter
John 10:1-10

Notes on This Reading

This Sunday is often referred to as Good Shepherd Sunday, tapping into the persistent scriptural metaphor that we all need a good shepherd, and that God provides that kind of pastoral leadership and care for us. Readings on this Sunday always include some portion of John 10. This year we read the first ten verses of that chapter, in which Jesus contrasts the shepherd of the sheep with those who are thieves. Jesus speaks of one who knows the sheep by name, a touching image of God's intimate love for each one of us. Doesn't it feel great when someone knows your name? Jesus mixes his metaphors a bit, and says, "I am the gate, the means of entry into the safety of the fold, the one who comes to bring abundant life, a great gift." If you have some extra time, read John 10 in its entirety. See what it has to teach you about a good shepherd.

Questions

1. What do you think it means that Jesus is the gatekeeper?

2. What does it mean that Jesus is the gate?

3. Who might be thieves and bandits?

4. In verse 10, Jesus promises to bring abundant life. What does abundant life look like for you? When have you experienced it? To what do you attribute it?

Fifth Sunday of Easter
John 14:1-14

Notes on This Reading

On this Sunday, we read a short portion of a long speech that Jesus gives to his disciples on the night before he died. So why do we read this in Easter season? Isn't it more appropriate for Holy Week? Perhaps it is because this passage is so filled with hope, even as it anticipates Jesus's death. Maybe that is why this passage is so often read at funerals. These verses speak of the promise that in death, life is changed, not ended. It speaks of God's preparation of a place for us. It encourages us to resist anxiety. And it calls us to discover the way, the truth and the life, in Jesus.

Questions

1. Why do you imagine that Jesus needed to tell the disciples not to be troubled? What might have made them anxious?

2. What does it mean to believe in God? Is it a matter of the head or the heart, or both?

3. Thomas asks: How can we know the way? Is that a question you have ever asked? What do you think of Jesus's answer?

4. Jesus says: If in my name you ask me for anything, I will do it. Do you believe that? What do you think Jesus meant by that?

Drawn to the Gospels • 86

Sixth Sunday of Easter
John 14:15-21

Notes on This Reading

We pick up where we left off last Sunday, as Jesus continues to coach his disciples before he leaves them, giving them counsel about how they are to live in the world after he has ascended. As we approach the day of Pentecost when we celebrate the gift of the Holy Spirit, we read about the promised gift of the Spirit—an advocate, a comforter. The word in Greek is *paraclete*, and it literally means one who comes along side. As the disciples await this divine presence, Jesus encourages them to keep his commandments, summed up in the call to love God and neighbor.

Questions

1. How do you think the disciples were feeling as they anticipated Jesus's departure?

2. Why is the Holy Spirit described as an advocate? When have you felt like you needed a spiritual advocate?

3. Jesus promises that the disciples will see him even when the world sees him no longer. What do you think he meant? How do we see Jesus today?

Ascension Day
Luke 24:44-53

Notes on This Reading

Forty days after Easter we celebrate Ascension Day, which always places it on a Thursday, so it may not get the attention that a feast that falls on a Sunday often gets. But it's an important story, described in both Luke's gospel and in the Acts of the Apostles. Jesus gives final instructions to his disciples. Then, in some mysterious way, he is taken up into heaven. In all its mystery, this feast day seeks to answer a few questions. What happened to Jesus after he was resurrected? What is next for the disciples?

Questions

1. What do you think is significant about the Feast of the Ascension? What would our faith be like if we didn't have this feast?

2. How would you feel if you were among the disciples that saw Jesus's ascent? What would be the range of emotions?

3. What was next for the disciples? How do you as a disciple move forward into an uncertain future? When have you had to do that?

WHAT WOULD JESUS PRAY?

That they may all be one...

Seventh Sunday of Easter
John 17:1-11

Notes on This Reading

We continue on this last Sunday of the Easter season to read from Jesus's long farewell address found in John 13–18. Chapter 17 allows us to eavesdrop on a prayer that Jesus offers, structured in three parts. Jesus prays first for himself, and for the ordeal he is about to undergo. Then he prays for the disciples who are with him, that they will be given strength. Finally, he prays for those who will come to faith through the disciples, which includes you and me. Read the whole chapter for insight into how Jesus prayed. And focus this year on that first part of the prayer, in which Jesus speaks of his desire to glorify God, and his deep care for his disciples as he leaves them. Ironically, the Gospel of John presents Jesus's death as his hour of glory, where God's sacrificial self-offering can be seen. That's quite a distinctive vision of glory.

Questions

1. What do you think you would pray for on the night before an experience like Jesus had?

2. What does it mean that Jesus glorified his Father while on earth? What does it mean to glorify another person?

3. Jesus prays for protection for his disciples. Why would they stand in need of protection?

4. What would you want Jesus to pray for you?

PENTECOST

Day of Pentecost
John 20:19-23

□ □ □

or John 7:37-39

Notes on These Readings

The early church adopted and adapted a Jewish feast, the feast of Pentecost, to note the day that the Holy Spirit descended on the disciples, filling them with power represented by fire and wind, giving them the gift of many languages, establishing them as a community that in short order would change the world. For that reason, it has often been called the birthday of the church. This particular day, recorded in chapter 2 of the Acts of the Apostles, was marked by extraordinary events, but the main point was that God was still very much present with the group of disciples, and that they had indeed received the power that they needed to make a difference.

Questions

1. Take time to read the story of Pentecost in Acts 2. How does it compare with the readings from the Gospel of John? What's similar? What's different?

2. In John's gospel, Jesus breathes on the disciples to share his power. In Acts, the power comes with a mighty wind. How have you received power to live a life of faith in the world? Where did that power come from?

3. What is important about breath and wind in the spiritual life? Note how many religious traditions focus on breath and wind.

Trinity Sunday
Matthew 28:16-20

Notes on This Reading

This Sunday is the only Sunday of the church year specifically dedicated to a doctrine or teaching of the church. After the great celebration of the gift of the Spirit, observed last week on Pentecost, this week we focus on the doctrine at the heart of our faith, the Trinity. It's a mysterious teaching for sure. It claims that God is one in three persons, a teaching reflected in the creeds of the church, a teaching implied in scripture but rarely explicitly set forth until several centuries after the church began. For this Sunday, we read the final verses of Matthew's gospel, known as the Great Commission. The disciples are instructed to bring the Good News to all people, baptizing them in the name of the Father and the Son and the Holy Spirit, language we still use in church, and one of the few places in the gospels where the Trinity is described so clearly. At its heart, this doctrine says that God is a community of love. The Good News is that we are invited to be part of that community. We are invited to join that holy conversation. What a privilege!

Questions

1. What does the doctrine of the Trinity mean to you? Why do you think it is important?

2. How would our faith be different if no such doctrine existed?

3. Of the three persons of the Trinity, is there one with which you resonate most strongly? Is there one which seems most mysterious?

4. What does it mean that God is by nature a community?

Proper 4
Matthew 7:21-29

Notes on This Reading

Earlier this year, we read selections from Jesus's Sermon on the Mount (Matthew 5–7). This morning, we come back to the conclusion of the sermon. Jesus sums it up by talking about those who hear his words and put them into action. They are like someone building a house on a solid foundation. Those who hear his words but don't put them into action are like someone building a house on sand. There's no solidity. It's an invitation to think about our lives and reflect on how we are building them, as we explore the ways that we put Jesus's teaching into action.

Questions

1. What do you think of the way Jesus concludes the Sermon on the Mount? What is the importance of putting his words into action? Where and how do you feel called to do that?

2. On what kind of foundation are you building? Do you ever feel like you are building on a foundation that is less than solid, that does not have staying power?

3. What are some ways you can build on a solid foundation this week? If you want to explore how other biblical writers used this image of building on a foundation, read 1 Corinthians 3.

Proper 5
Matthew 9:9-13, 18-26

Notes on This Reading

Two very different stories are offered in this passage. We begin with the call of Matthew, to whom is attributed authorship of this gospel. He served as a tax collector, which makes him less than popular among his people because he collaborated with Roman oppressors to make a profit off of his neighbors. None of that stopped Jesus from inviting him into a new life. Note that when Matthew heard Jesus's call, he immediately followed, a remarkable demonstration of faith and courage. Perhaps it's an indication that deep down, Matthew wanted a new life. He wanted a new line of work. The story of Matthew is linked to two miraculous healings, the raising of Jairus's daughter from the dead and the healing of a woman who had been sick for twelve years. In each case, great and courageous faith was exhibited.

Questions

1. What do you think of Matthew's response to Jesus's instruction, "Follow me"? If Jesus said that to you, what would that mean for your life? What does it mean to follow Jesus these days?

2. Why was Jesus criticized for eating with tax collectors and sinners? Who should he have been eating with?

3. What do Jairus and the woman suffering from hemorrhages have in common? What do they have in common with Matthew? What do they all have to teach us about the spiritual life?

Proper 6
Matthew 9:35–10:8 (9-23)

Notes on This Reading

We read in this passage about Jesus's plans to send out his disciples. That commissioning comes in response to his regard for the crowd of people who had gathered to hear his teaching. Matthew tells us that Jesus had compassion on the crowd, because they were harassed and helpless, like sheep without a shepherd. Jesus could probably say that about us, too. With an eye on a plentiful harvest (i.e., lots of work to do), Jesus sends out the disciples with specific instructions. He tells them to travel light, to offer his work of healing wherever they go. He tells them to extend peace in those places, and if they are not welcomed, to move on. If your church chooses to read the longer version of this gospel, you'll hear how Jesus tells these disciples that it won't be easy, and that they'll run into opposition. This passage offers a beautiful expression of what Dietrich Bonhoeffer called the cost of discipleship.

Questions

1. What does the word compassion mean to you? Religious scholar Karen Armstrong describes it as the central virtue of all major world religions. How did Jesus exhibit compassion? When have you experienced compassion? When have you shown it?

2. What lessons do we as disciples have from Jesus's instructions to his disciples?

3. When Jesus says the harvest is plentiful, what does that mean to you? What is the holy work that lies before you?

Proper 7
Matthew 10:24-39

Notes on This Reading

Jesus continues his rather hard-hitting teaching, encouraging his disciples as they go out to face opposition. If he was going to experience this kind of challenge, so would his followers. It's a message meant not only for the twelve disciples who walked with Jesus, but for those who would follow him in later generations. He reminds the disciples that God cares for them. Jesus invites them to stay strong and to stay true to their calling. But he also doesn't want them to operate under any illusion that he is promising an easy pathway. He says he comes to bring not peace, but a sword. He notes that he will divide families against each other. He asks them to take up their cross. With all of that, it may be surprising that he had any followers at all!

Questions

1. How do you think Jesus's listeners responded to this challenging teaching?

2. What do you think it might mean that Jesus comes to bring a sword rather than peace? Does that fit with your image of Jesus?

3. In what sense does Jesus divide families?

4. Can you think of ways that people find their life by losing it?

5. Can you think of ways that people can take up their cross these days?

Proper 8
Matthew 10:40-42

Notes on This Reading

The theme in today's gospel is welcome. In this short passage, we get a big message: If we welcome Christ's servants or followers, we are actually welcoming Christ. When we do that, we are welcoming the one who sent Christ. It's a truth reflected in baptism, that we seek and serve Christ in all persons. That welcome can be a very simple act—a gift of cold water to someone who may in the world's eyes have little significance. But it is something that each one of us is called to do. Even better, it's something that each one of us can do. That's a pretty good reason to work on our welcome.

Questions

1. How can you practice welcome toward those who come in Christ's name?

2. How is your community of faith doing with its welcome? What is getting in the way of a more effective and open spirit of welcome in your community?

3. What can you do this week that is comparable to giving a cup of cold water to someone else?

Proper 9
Matthew 11:16-19, 25-30

Notes on This Reading

Jesus continues to contend with opponents, who never seem to be happy with him, no matter what he does. They complained that John the Baptist was too much of a downer. They complain that Jesus is a glutton and a drunkard, basically a party animal. He couldn't win with those folks. With all that in mind, Jesus gives thanks that he is embraced and understood by the common people. He ends with a beautiful invitation included in the liturgy in our Prayer Book (see page 332, the Comfortable Words in Holy Eucharist Rite I). Jesus invites any who are weary and heavy laden to come to him, to take his yoke on them, claiming that his yoke is easy and his burden is light. In the Hebrew Scriptures, the yoke was often described as the law, the teaching of the scripture. Jesus invites hearers to take his teaching, his law of love, upon them and to find that it is not burdensome. Indeed, it has the power to lift life's burdens.

Questions

1. The Bible is filled with stories of folks who never seem quite satisfied. The children of Israel wandered in the wilderness for forty years, always asking God: What have you done for me lately? We see that in today's gospel. Can you identify with that dynamic at all? Have you seen it at work in communities of faith?

2. What do you think might serve as an antidote to this kind of complaining or dissatisfied spirit?

3. How does Jesus give rest?

4. What does it mean to you that Jesus's yoke is easy and his burden is light? What is his yoke? In the Jewish tradition, the teaching or the law was described as a yoke. How does this help us understand what Jesus was talking about?

Proper 10
Matthew 13:1-9, 18-23

Notes on This Reading

With this passage, we begin a third discourse in Matthew's gospel, offering more teaching from Jesus. This time it's a series of parables, one of the wonderful ways Jesus got his message across. If you want to appreciate his genius as a teacher, try your hand at writing a parable. It's not easy. Today we read one of the lengthier ones; it is distinctive because Jesus offers an explanation for what the parable means. In that way, it becomes something of an allegory. In Matthew's vision, it sounds as if the seed that is being sown is the word. As that seed falls on the ground, it meets with different fate depending on where it lands. The parable may well be an explanation for why some people come to faith and why others don't, one of life's great mysteries.

Questions

1. Why do you think Jesus told parables? What do you think of storytelling as a teaching method? What are its advantages? What are the challenges?

2. In this parable, who do you think is the sower? What is the seed?

3. Do you recognize any of the various kinds of soil: that with no depth, that with thorns, that which birds took the seed away?

4. What has helped you grow spiritually? What has gotten in the way?

5. What do you take as a lesson from this parable?

Proper 11
Matthew 13:24-30, 36-43

Notes on This Reading

We continue this week with another parable, related to the parable of the sower and the seed from last week. Here we read about a field where good wheat and lousy weeds grow up together. Apparently, no one is sure how that happened. How did good and bad get planted in the same field? Workers want to pull out the bad and leave the good, but the farmer says let it be. Trust that the future will take care of what needs to be taken care of.

Questions

1. How would you preach on this parable? What do you think is the point of this story?

2. What might be the good wheat that is growing?

3. What would be the weeds?

4. To what mystery does this parable point? What lessons from this parable might you apply to your own life?

Proper 12
Matthew 13:31-33, 44-52

Notes on This Reading

We continue to explore Jesus's parables. A parable can be lengthy or quite short. In today's passage, several parables are grouped together. The first two underscore the biblical theme that great things can emerge from small beginnings. A mustard seed grows into a tree that can provide shelter for all the birds. The parable about yeast echoes that same theme. It only takes a little influence to make a big change. The parables about treasure in a field and a pearl of great price speak about what we value, where we put our treasure, and what we will do to attain it. The parable of the fish speaks of the breadth of God's reach, a message of expansive inclusiveness. Put them all together and we get a powerful vision of God's reign.

Questions

1. What does the mustard seed parable say to you? What difference can a small amount make? Where have you seen that dynamic at work?

2. How about the parable of the yeast? Can you think of a time when a small influence had great effect?

3. Have you ever pursued a pearl of great price, giving up everything for a particular goal?

4. What does the great catch of fish say about faith?

5. Do you think these four parables belong together, or are they conveying totally different messages?

Proper 13
Matthew 14:13-21

Notes on This Reading

On this day, we read one of the stories that appears in each of the gospels, the miraculous feeding of five thousand people. It's certainly a story about meeting a need of physical hunger, but it's also much more. It's about the way that God provides a banquet. It's about how a small offering can make a big difference. And it's about the way Jesus regards all of us. As in other gospel accounts, Matthew tells us that Jesus looked out on the crowd that had gathered in a deserted place and he had compassion on them. Compassion, which literally means "suffering with," is a hallmark of Jesus's ministry, as he comes among us, endures what we as humans endure, and holds the promise that he will meet our needs, with plenty leftover.

Questions

1. Does this story have something to tell us about meeting physical hunger in our world? Where do you run into that kind of need?

2. When have you experienced spiritual hunger? How has that hunger been met?

3. Have you ever felt that you didn't have enough resources to meet a need?

4. When have you been on the receiving end of compassionate regard? When have you had opportunity to show compassion to someone else?

Proper 14
Matthew 14:22-33

Notes on This Reading

As we noted in last week's reading, each of the gospels tells the story of the feeding of the five thousand. They all follow that up with Jesus crossing the sea in the middle of a storm, and then calming it. Matthew's gospel adds a twist: it is the only gospel that shares the story of Peter seeking to join Jesus in walking on the water. On the one hand, it's a remarkable witness to Peter's faith, that he says to Jesus: "If it is you, let me walk on water, too." On the other hand, it's kind of a crazy thing to try to do. Who walks on water? As Peter steps out, courageously putting one foot over the gunwale, and then the other, apparently he loses his nerve. He loses his focus on Jesus. He is both rescued and reprimanded for his doubts. The story ends with the seas calmed and with the disciples in the boat worshipping Jesus.

Questions

1. What is the significance of Jesus walking on the water? What does that strange power suggest about Jesus?

2. What do we learn about Peter in this story? What did it take for him to step out onto the water?

3. Have you ever had to do something that felt like that? Have you ever started something and then lost your courage?

4. What does it mean that Jesus has the power to calm the seas? Have you ever had storms calmed in your life?

Proper 15
Matthew 15:(10-20) 21-28

Notes on This Reading

This Sunday, you may or may not hear this whole passage in church. The reading begins with Jesus's response to the legalism of his religious opponents. He makes the point that life with God is not about the rules. It's not about external legislation that governs our behavior. It's about what is in the heart. It's about love. This teaching is linked to a remarkable story in which Jesus meets a Canaanite woman who asks for help. This woman was an outsider. At first, Jesus resists helping her, claiming that his ministry is primarily to the Jewish people. To our ears, that sounds harsh, but the woman persists and Jesus seems to change his mind. Maybe he was testing her. Maybe he actually came to see things in a new way, which is a sign of Jesus's humanity, and probably something each one of us should learn to do.

Questions

1. In your experience, how much of religious life is about rules? Have you ever encountered leaders, religious or otherwise, who seem to be blind guides?

2. What do you think of the way Jesus responded to the Canaanite woman? Was he harsh? Was he testing her?

3. What does she teach us about encounters with Jesus? What does she model for us as disciples? What if we didn't have this story in the gospels?

4. Do you think Jesus changed his mind? Do you think he was initially wrong? If Jesus did indeed change his mind, how does that fit with your understanding of who he was?

Proper 16
Matthew 16:13-20

Notes on This Reading

We noted in the foreword of the book that one of the ways to look at the gospels is to ask, "Who is Jesus in this story?" We didn't make that question up. In fact, we can trace it all the way back to Jesus himself, who gathered his disciples and asked their sense of popular perception about him. What are the people saying? It may be the first recorded instance of public opinion polling. But after the disciples give their answers, Jesus turns the question on them, asking "Who do you say that I am?" It's a question meant for those first disciples, but also meant for each one of us. We each have to decide how we might answer. Peter speaks for each one of us, affirming that Jesus is the Messiah. This event is so important that in the church calendar, there's a feast to celebrate this story, called the Feast of the Confession of Peter, observed on January 18. Once Peter makes that confession, he's told in Matthew's gospel that he will be the rock on which the church will be built. Jesus grants Peter the keys to the kingdom. It may seem that Peter was hardly a rock, but if Jesus could use him to build his church, maybe he can use us as well.

Questions

1. What are the variety of answers you might get if you asked the general public: Who do people say that Jesus is?

2. How would you answer Jesus's question: Who do you say that I am? What in your life has helped to shape your answer?

3. What kind of rock was Peter on which to build the church? What do you think Jesus meant that he would be receiving the keys of the kingdom?

Proper 17
Matthew 16:21-28

Notes on This Reading

Today's story builds on last week's reading in which Jesus has described Peter as the rock on which the church will be built. But then Jesus goes on to tell Peter and the disciples that along with this new job, this new ministry, will come challenge. Jesus tells his group of followers that the road ahead will involve great suffering. Peter, a disciple who apparently never has an unexpressed thought, rebukes Jesus for talking this way. Jesus, who just recently called Peter a rock, now tells Peter, "Get behind me, Satan."

Questions

1. Do you think Jesus is hard on Peter? What was wrong with what Peter suggested? How would Peter's comment be identified with Satan?

2. What does it mean to deny oneself and take up the cross? Have you ever had to do that?

3. What does it mean to find your life by losing it? Have you ever seen that dynamic at work?

Proper 18
Matthew 18:15-20

Notes on This Reading

Matthew's gospel is the one that talks most about life in the church. The Greek word for church is *ecclesia*, from which we get words like ecclesiastical. The word literally means "called out," which suggests a community that is to be distinctive. In this passage, we see that distinctive quality at work in a very practical way, as Jesus presents a process by which disagreements are resolved. Newsflash: conflict in church is nothing new. Jesus's teaching outlines a process by which issues can be addressed in ways that preserve the dignity of all involved. It begins with respect for privacy. Then in steps, the process broadens engagement as needed, until the whole community may be involved. This reading highlights that the church is empowered with a ministry of forgiveness, reconciliation, and restoration. The need for this kind of ministry was apparently significant in the first century. It still is needed.

Questions

1. What do you think of the process outlined for dealing with injuries in the community? Have you ever seen this at work?

2. Why is it important to add witnesses along the way?

3. Jesus promises to be present where two or three are gathered in his name. How does this affect your own gatherings?

Proper 19
Matthew 18:21-35

Notes on This Reading

The theme of reconciliation continues, as Peter asks how far he has to carry this forgiveness business. Peter seems to think he's been quite magnanimous if he agrees to forgive someone seven times. Jesus says that is only the beginning. Forgiveness must be offered seven times seventy times. In other words, there's no point in setting limits on how often we forgive. To make his point about forgiveness, Jesus tells a story about a man who is forgiven a great debt. That same man in short order refuses to forgive a small debt owed to him. It ends up being a harsh parable of judgment, making the point that the best way to acknowledge our own appreciation of forgiveness is to extend forgiveness to others. Maybe that's what the line in the Lord's Prayer is talking about when it asks, "Forgive us our trespasses as we forgive those who trespass against us."

Questions

1. Does the unlimited forgiveness that Jesus demands seem like a good thing? Could it seem like enabling?

2. Bishop Desmond Tutu of South Africa wrote a book entitled, *No Future Without Forgiveness.* Why do you think that forgiveness is so important in the spiritual life, in faith communities?

3. What do you find difficult about forgiveness? How are you able to extend forgiveness? Can you remember a time when someone extended forgiveness to you? How did that make you feel? Did it make you more inclined to forgive others, or less so?

Proper 20
Matthew 20:1-16

Notes on This Reading

This is one of the stories Jesus told that can get preachers in trouble. Many people don't like this parable because it violates any sense of fairness. It would certainly be a hard way to run a business. But in its evocative and provocative nature, the story speaks powerfully about grace. Wherever we are in the spiritual journey, whether we've been at it for a lifetime or have just begun, we can find ourselves on the receiving end of God's lavish love. Was it fair for the folks who worked all day in the hot sun to get paid the same as those who started at a quarter to five? It is probably not fair, but the parable makes the point that grace is unmerited, given freely according to God's will and not as a measure of our own efforts, nor a reflection of our merit or value. God can be generous with whom God wants to be generous. All of that has already been established by God's love.

Questions

1. Who do you relate to in this story? The folks who worked all day and resented folks who came later? Or the folks who came on the scene at the end of the day?

2. What would you say is the point of this parable? Why do you think Jesus told it?

3. When have you experienced grace, which has been described as unmerited favor? When have you shown it?

4. Why do you think people often react unfavorably to this story when it shows up in the lectionary? How would you advise a preacher to preach on it?

Proper 21
Matthew 21:23-32

Notes on This Reading

One of the great themes of the gospels has to do with Jesus's encounter with the religious authorities of his day. Earlier in this chapter we read about Jesus's triumphal entry into Jerusalem, a story we heard on Palm Sunday. The crowds may have been excited by this grand procession and the spontaneous acclaim of the people. The religious authorities, not so much. They want to know where Jesus got the authority to teach as he did, to do the things he was doing. He is clearly operating outside of the system that put them in their place of privilege. They don't like that, as it challenges the system that gave them power. Jesus refuses to get into an argument with his opponents, but, as he often does, he tells a parable that speaks about the different ways that people react to authority.

Questions

1. Why do you think the religious authorities were worried about Jesus? What in them and in their way of life did he threaten?

2. It's been said that Jesus came to comfort the afflicted and afflict the comfortable. Do you see him doing that in this passage? Have you seen him do that in your life?

3. When Jesus told the parable of the two sons, where do you see yourself in that parable?

Proper 22
Matthew 21:33-46

Notes on This Reading

Jesus continues to get his point across with the use of parables, a brilliant way to teach. He challenges his listeners in a way that makes them rethink things. In this case, he tells a parable about wicked tenants, a parable that dawns on the religious authorities of the day as the story unfolds. The parable describes a landowner who has a well-established vineyard managed by his tenants. The landowner sends servants to collect the produce. A series of messengers are sent, each of which is treated roughly—some beaten, some killed. The landlord finally sends his son, convinced that the tenants will honor him. The tenants kill the son, operating under the impression that they will inherit the vineyard. Let's just say it's not the clearest logic. Jesus then interprets the parable to show that the religious leaders of the day are like those wicked tenants. The chief priests and Pharisees realize Jesus is talking about them, and they are not happy. They want to arrest Jesus. The tension as we move toward the story of Holy Week is mounting.

Questions

1. Who do you think the landlord, the tenants, the servants, and the son represent?

2. Do the actions of the tenants make any sense? Do we sometimes act in similar ways, ways that defy logic?

3. Do we ever confuse our role as tenants or stewards with the role of landlord or owner?

4. Why would the religious leaders be so upset with the telling of this story? Would religious leaders today react in a similar fashion?

Proper 23
Matthew 22:1-14

Notes on This Reading

We continue to be taught by Jesus through his use of parables—stories that make us think differently about the world. One of the great themes in these parables has to do with wedding banquets and the invitation to God's feast. In this story, those who had been invited make light of the invitation. Others even abuse the servants who extend the invitation. In response, the king exacts judgment on those who refused to come. Then he invites folks who would never have been invited. The parable ends with a strange twist. The king sees someone at the feast without the proper wedding garment. The king has him thrown out, saying many are called but few are chosen, which makes what was otherwise a parable of grace also a parable of judgment.

Questions

1. What do you think was the point Jesus was trying to make in this story? Do you have an idea who invited guests might be? What do you make of their strange, ungrateful response to the invitation?

2. Who do you think are the folks who might have been included in the banquet after those who were invited refuse the invitation?

3. What sense can you make of this last part of the passage which describes a guest who gets tossed out? What might that wedding garment represent? Listen closely to sermons this Sunday. See if the preacher gives you any clues, or if she or he avoids this part.

Proper 24
Matthew 22:15-22

Notes on This Reading

Once more, people are setting a trap for Jesus, trying to get him to say that he either supports Caesar or doesn't. Either way, he could wind up in trouble. He would not want to run up against the violent, oppressive Romans. He would not want to be seen as a collaborator with them, either. So when the issue of whether to pay taxes comes up, Jesus turns the tables on them. He asks whose image is on the coin, and then states that they should give to Caesar the things that are Caesar's, and give to God the things that are God's. Dorothy Day put her own spin on this story in this way: if we rendered to God the things that are God's, there would be little left over for Caesar. The story makes us think about what we owe to temporal authorities and what we owe to the God of creation, who made us all.

Questions

1. What were the risks for Jesus in the various ways he could answer the question put before him? How exactly was it a test?

2. What does this story tell us about our responsibility as citizens and our responsibility as followers of Jesus?

3. Do those two things ever come into conflict for you?

4. Who are the Caesars in our world today?

Proper 25
Matthew 22:34-46

Notes on This Reading

As we come closer to Holy Week in Matthew's gospel, the tension is mounting. Once again, Jesus confronts the religious authorities. We read, this week, that a lawyer comes to test Jesus, asking which commandment is the greatest. Favoring one commandment over another could get him into trouble. In response to the question, Jesus reaches back into his knowledge of scripture and answers that the greatest commandment is really twofold: love of God and love of neighbor. As one rabbi put it, everything else is commentary. Jesus then turns the table, with a question about what the religious leaders think of the Messiah. Could he be the Son of David? If so, why does David call him Lord? No one was able to answer, and Matthew tells us that Jesus's skillful responses quieted his opponents.

Questions

1. Why do you think that Jesus was constantly being put to the test? What were his opponents trying to accomplish?

2. Jesus was asked to name one great commandment. In response, he offers two. How are love of God and love of neighbor related? Can you have one without the other?

3. Why do you think Jesus's opponents were stumped by his comments about David? How do you think they felt?

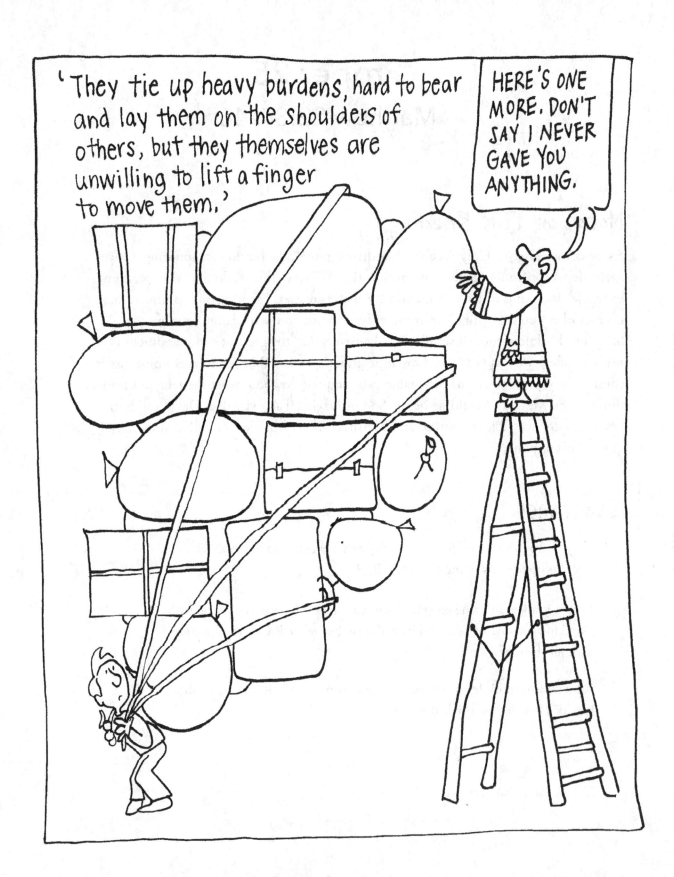

Proper 26
Matthew 23:1-12

Notes on This Reading

With this reading, we begin the fifth discourse, another collection of Jesus's teachings offered in Matthew. And as we come closer to the climax of the gospel described in the story of Holy Week and Easter, the tension between Jesus and his opponents mounts. The irony that his fiercest opponents are the most religious people of his day is striking. As Jesus talks to the crowds and to his disciples, he tells them to do what these religious leaders say, but not to follow their actions. Those actions are marked by hypocrisy, the imposition of rigorous religious standards that they themselves would not or could not fulfill. Jesus highlights their interest in having places of honor, and counters that the greatest will be the servant, that those who exalt themselves will be humbled and that those who humble themselves will be exalted.

Questions

1. What warning does Jesus give about religious figures in high-profile public places?

2. How do you think the scribes and Pharisees felt about what Jesus had to say?

3. Why does greatness come with servanthood?

4. Who do you know who exhibits humility? What is it about that person that conveys that spirit? How do you think one arrives at a place of humility? What does it take to get there?

Proper 27
Matthew 25:1-13

Notes on This Reading

As we move toward the end of the year, and as we continue to move toward Holy Week, the ominous spirit of warning gets stronger. This week, that spirit is conveyed in the parable of ten maidens gathered in expectation of a wedding. Five of the maidens come prepared with plenty of oil for their lamps, to be carried in the procession from the bride's house to the groom's house. Five of the maidens didn't plan ahead and didn't bring enough oil for their lamps. Consequently, they have to run off and find some oil and they miss the arrival of the bridegroom. The meaning of the parable is summed up in a call to preparedness, to keep awake. The parable may well be something like "Coming Attractions" for the upcoming season of Advent, with its repeated call to be ready, to be awake, to be mindful, watching for the arrival of the Son of God.

Questions

1. If you had to preach on this parable, what would be your focus?

2. Who might the bridegroom represent? How are we to be ready for the arrival of the bridegroom?

3. Who is responsible for having enough oil?

4. What helps you stay alert? What helps you with mindfulness? What are the things that cause distraction for you?

Proper 28
Matthew 25:14-30

Notes on This Reading

This week, we build on a series of parables about being prepared for end times. In today's parable, Jesus makes the point that we have all been given gifts. In Jesus's time, a talent was a measure of money. In the parable, one servant is given five talents, equivalent to 30,000 denarii. One denarii represented a day's wage for a laborer, so we're talking about a lot of money. Another servant is given two talents. A third is given just one. The first two servants invest the gifts. They make a profit, which is returned to the master. They made use of what they had been given. The third does not, and so is condemned by the master, with the warning that to those who have been given, more will be given. But for those who have little, what they have will be taken away. It's a parable of judgment—a call to use gifts and talents we have been given and not to hoard them out of fear.

Questions

1. What does this parable say about gifts we've been given? What does it mean that we're not all given the same? Is that fair?

2. A talent in biblical times was a measure of money. But in our day it can be a lot of things. Think about the talents you've been given. How are you using them?

3. Take note of the collect read this Sunday: "Blessed Lord, who caused all holy Scriptures to be written for our learning: Grant us so to hear them, read, mark, learn, and inwardly digest them, that we may embrace and ever hold fast the blessed hope of everlasting life, which you have given us in our Savior Jesus Christ; who lives and reigns with you and the Holy Spirit, one God, for ever and ever. Amen."

4. It calls us to pay attention to scripture, which is the point of this book. And note why we are to do that. It is in order that we might have hope. Is it your experience that the scriptures give us hope?

Proper 29
Matthew 25:31-46

Notes on This Reading

We come to the end of the church year, with a Sunday focused on Christ the King. As you may have noted in recent weeks, a foreboding tone of judgment can be detected in our readings, culminating in this story of the final judgment. A king gathers all the nations before him and renders judgment. The king separates people as a shepherd would separate sheep from goats and makes the following distinction: The sheep, those commended and embraced by the King, are those who fed the hungry, visited prisoners, attended to those who were sick. The goats are those who were indifferent to those kinds of needs. This passage again, a parable of judgment, gives warrant for Jesus's disciples to discover Christ the King in those who are the neediest.

Questions

1. When you think of Jesus, do you think of him as a king who will render judgment?

2. Notice that both sheep and goats are surprised that they have either been serving or ignoring the king. What does that say about service to those in need in our world?

3. As we come to the end of the year and begin anew next Sunday, what does this parable say to us as individuals and to our church? Are we more like sheep or more like goats? Or do we have a bit of both in each of us?

IN CONCLUSION

It has been a privilege to take on this project. It has given me renewed appreciation for the Gospel of Matthew, especially the great collections of Jesus's teaching. After years of preaching on lectionary texts, the opportunity to reflect on the whole year brought me to a new and refreshed gratitude for the life and ministry of Jesus. His guiding presence as teacher shines through these passages. As these readings have spoken to me in new ways, I hope and pray that they will move your heart as well.

—The Rev. Jay Sidebotham

I love to tell the story of unseen things above,
Of Jesus and his glory, of Jesus and his love.
I love to tell the story because I know it is true
It satisfies my longing as nothing else can do.

I love to tell the story, 'twill be my theme in glory,
To tell the old, old story of Jesus and his love.

I love to tell the story for those who know it best
Seem hungering and thirsting to hear it like the rest,
And when in scenes of glory I sing the new, new song,
'Twill be the old, old story, that I have loved so long.